Joyful Journey
Finding your way over the wall and toward your possibilities

Pamela Spivey

Debi,
Your light shines
through your
Joyful Journey
Pam Spivey

Joyful Journey

ISBN: 9781095577295

DEDICATION

This book is dedicated to all who have crossed my path
and helped me reach this moment in life. I am truly grateful for your
wise counsel, loving kindness, and never-ending support. This
journey, my story, could not have been written without you.

CONTENTS

ACKNOWLEDGMENTS

I couldn't have accomplished writing this book without the love and support of my husband. Stowe you encouraged me every step of the way.

To our son, Kyle you are wise beyond your years! Thank you for researching and then educating me on the ways of the worldwide web. You made what was so difficult in my brain, so simple to execute.

Sweet Allison, thank you for designing exactly what I had envisioned. You make the book come to life with your illustrations!

Mom and Dad, I know you are smiling down from heaven. Thank you for loving me and laying the foundation for this joyful journey.

Donna, thank you for helping me find the way back to joy when I thought it was impossible. You were able to reach me and teach me how important it is to care for myself first. You opened my eyes to the possibilities again.

Kim, what can I say but, thank you from the bottom of my heart! You coached me and cared for me and for that, I am truly grateful. Words really can't express all that I have learned about myself during our weekly coaching calls. You kept me accountable and moving forward. You challenged me to expand my thinking and stretch beyond what I perceived as possible.

For all my family and friends, thank you for believing in me and praying for me when I wasn't myself. Your love and prayers lifted me up and over the wall.

Now I delight in the many blessings God has provided and look forward to what's next!

Joyful Journey

1
THE JOURNEY

"The journey in between what you once were and who you are now becoming is where the dance of life really takes place."

Barbara De Angelis

The journey begins like this…

Once upon a time there was a little girl that looked at life through broken glasses. Not seeing what was ahead, but instead, looking down at the ground. Not understanding why she was being called to the office one day in first grade. Not comprehending the significance of her friend saying "I'll never see you again" as she left the classroom. Or why she and her mom, brother and sister were driving away from the school with all their belongings packed in a U-Haul trailer hooked to the back of our car.

That little girl was me and as we traveled north, I learned my parents were getting a divorce. I may never understand the reasons, but I do know that my mom was doing the best she could for us as a family. She loved us so much and wanted a better life for me, my brother and sister. I also know (through years of therapy) that my having adult-like responsibilities so early in life was quite a burden. An original latch key kid with multiple responsibilities, I didn't have much time for playing and having fun. I had to make sure chores got done, homework was started and everyone was taken care of. I was the 'second mom' as my brother would sarcastically call me. These responsibilities shaped my actions, responses, and thoughts growing up. I became the pleaser, the perfectionist, the performer, and the 'Pam' everyone needed. My mom often introduced me with much pride as being "born an adult". I know now, I really just wanted to be a kid.

Fast forward this journey to January 16, 2015…

I'm sitting in my boss's office getting ready to receive my annual evaluation. But I can't concentrate. I'm so tired! I haven't slept much the past few days. Getting home late and going to work early has been the norm and arguing with my husband is a daily routine. I'm behind on projects, my inbox has 352 unread messages, and hundreds more of opened emails that needed to be answered. The professional organization of which I am now the president has a board meeting coming up with program deadlines looming. My husband just landed his dream job which has him traveling every week. I've let my friends down by canceling coffee, lunch and 'girls not out' because I'm so busy! I've become clumsy and fallen a couple of times walking across campus to different meetings. Could it be I'm thinking about all the things I need to do instead of watching where I'm going? My staff start their conversations with me saying 'I know you are so busy, but…''. On top of all of this, my mom has been diagnosed with atrial fibrillation and congested heart failure.

I'm seriously wondering what made me think that I could be a leader, a wife, a daughter, a friend, an adult. I'm so tired!

Before I knew what was happening I started crying. Everybody knows you don't cry at work, right? I was crying uncontrollably in my boss's office telling her how sorry I was for letting her down, not doing my job well, and for not telling her sooner. All I could see were my faults, failures, my inability to do anything right. What a mess!

I was beyond overwhelmed and exhausted. I was pouring myself into everything I thought I was supposed to do, what I should do, what I must do, that I didn't see the wall until it was crashing down on me.

The next thing I remember is sitting in the psychologist's office in Employee Assistance - still crying - she calls a doctor (who soon becomes my psychiatrist) and I'm seen within the hour. Severe depression, acute anxiety and a recommendation of 6 weeks of intensive outpatient therapy… My leave of absence has begun.

Almost 4 years now have passed since that moment and I'm writing to you from the other side of the wall. Hoping that sharing one word, one thing, one part of my story helps you away from the wall and toward your possibilities. There is a way up and over, a way to restore your joy and move forward.

There is work to be done and not all of it will be easy. As a matter of fact, some of it will be really hard! But I know you can do it. You are strong enough! I'm the hand reaching over the wall to help you.

Take my hand. We can do this together!

Each chapter of this book describes one essential thought, practice, or skill I've learned along my journey. I'll share stories, quotes and activities that I hope will help you make your way back to joy. There will be questions for you to reflect on and even act on right in the moment. I encourage you to write down your thoughts. By writing them down you are releasing them, acknowledging them and even letting some of them go. Journaling became my first baby step back to joy. I learned to release negative thoughts and move forward ever so cautiously, one incremental step at a time.

You may notice that each chapter has a one word title. This is by design. Pick which word resonates with you in the moment. Read them in the order you choose. The chapters of our lives don't necessarily follow any semblance of order, why should this book be any different.

O.K., it's time. I'm here to help. Move away from that wall and toward your possibilities. Let's face the obstacles, grow from them, bounce back and while doing so, consider it all Joy!

2
RESILIENCE

*"Joy, collected over time, fuels resilience - ensuring
we'll have reservoirs of emotional strength when hard times do happen"*

Brené Brown

There are times in our lives when remaining in the present circumstance requires us to reach within for strength, courage and a warrior-like attitude. It may be a battle for your health and wellbeing or it may a battle for someone or something that is very important to you. Many times in our career and our personal life we are called to be warriors. When we are, we have to stand our ground, fight passionately for ourselves, and even take on what we think at the time is insurmountable.

 After speaking with a friend of mine who was going through a difficult time, I was drawn to explore this warrior strength a little more. I'm obsessed with definitions, so the first thing I did was 'google' the definition of warrior. Merriam Webster defines warrior as "a person who shows or has shown great vigor, courage". Another source was similar, "known for having courage and skill; a brave or experienced soldier". Warriors are action oriented. Warrior souls tend to see life in terms of confrontations and rising to the challenge. There are causes to serve, struggles to overcome, and yes, battles to be won. Warriors like to be on the front line with their trusted colleagues, and strongly value both courage and loyalty.

I've seen many examples of individuals and groups charging to the frontline, demonstrating courage and fighting the good fight. One thing I believe each of these warriors have is resilience. Resilience means facing life's difficulties with courage and patience, refusing to give up. It is the quality of character that allows a person or group of people to bounce back from hardships and traumas. One psychology expert states that resilience is rooted in a tenacity of spirit, a determination to embrace all that makes life worth living even in the face of overwhelming odds. When we have a clear sense of identity and purpose, we are more resilient, because we can hold fast to our vision of a better future.

Much of our resilience comes from community - from the relationships that allow us to lean on each other for support when we need it. Community and making connections was instrumental in my life when I needed it most. The relationships with close family members, friends and others are important. Accepting help and support from those who care about you and will listen to you strengthens resilience. It was hard accepting help, but critical to my bouncing back.

On June 12, 2007 I was diagnosed with breast cancer. Up until that moment, I thought cancer happened to other people, not me. I couldn't believe it, wouldn't believe it! But after talking to the oncologist, I realized that I had cancer, I needed surgery followed by chemotherapy and radiation to eradicate it from my body.

I remember calling my mom to tell her and she responded with a calmness and peace only God could provide. You know, it's that peace that passes all understanding. But even with that peace, I was reluctant to ask for help. When our Sunday School class wanted to prepare meals and help around the house during my treatments, I declined. I was an strong adult. I didn't want to burden anyone. I was used to helping others, first as the eldest child in the family and then as a registered nurse working with moms and babies. How could I ask for help? I was the caregiver, not receiver? My mom helped me understand when she said, "don't rob them of their joy". So I asked and accepted help.

My friend Pattie brought flowers each week to brighten my days. Hot meals and cold applesauce (best thing ever when nausea set in) showed up daily. My sweet husband kept me entertained during chemo and shaved my head when hair began falling out. Frieda, my friend, coordinated everything at work and made a neckless for me with beads representing each milestone along the way. So many friends and colleagues shared their thoughts and prayers. My professors and classmates in graduate school - oh yeah, did I mention I was in graduate school when diagnosed – supported me wholeheartedly when I was too stubborn to take a break.

You can't always change the stressful events that happen, but you can choose how you respond to them. Resiliency was fostered and grown as a result of seeking help during this difficult time in my life. Bouncing back with joy was possible because of human connections.

Do you have a network of friends or colleagues to go to when you are in stress?

Take a moment right now to write their names below. If you answered no, that's okay. List 2 connections (a person, a family member, a support group) you'll make this week.

If one of your friends or family members needed help today, what would you do?

Think back to a time when you were going through a difficult situation. What did you do?

Where did the courage and tenacity come from? How did you bounce back?

Give yourself a little joy!

3
POSITIVITY

"Stay positive and trust your journey"

Pam Spivey

Over the past several years I have been very purposeful in reframing my thoughts and responses to positive thinking. I even revised my mission statement, "to express joy in everything I do and spread joy around me through a positive, wholehearted lifestyle filled with gratitude".

Did you know that positive thinking is about more than just being happy or displaying an upbeat attitude? Positive thoughts can actually create real value in your life and help you build skills that last much longer than a smile.

Barbara Fredrickson, a positive psychology researcher at the University of North Carolina describes in her research the powerful impact of positive thinking on your work, your health, and your life.

Fredrickson tested the impact of positive emotions on the brain by setting up a little experiment. During this experiment, she divided her research subjects into five groups and showed each group different film clips. Group 1 and 2 were shown clips that created positive emotions – *joy* and *contentment*. Group 3 (the control group) saw images that were neutral and produced no significant emotion. Groups 4 and 5 were shown clips that created negative emotions – *fear* and *anger*.

After the clips, each participant was asked to imagine themselves in a situation where similar feelings would arise and to write down what they would do.

Each participant was handed a piece of paper with 20 blank lines that started with the phrase, "I would like to..."

Participants who saw images of fear and anger wrote down the fewest responses. The participants who saw images of joy and contentment, wrote down a significantly higher number of actions that they would take, even when compared to the neutral group.

Dr. Fredrickson's discovery is when you are experiencing positive emotions like joy, contentment, and love, you will see more possibilities in your life. These findings were among the first that suggested positive emotions broaden your sense of possibility and open your mind up to more options.

Then why do we often focus on negative thoughts? Could it be we're wired to respond that way?

Okay, you all have probably heard some version of this story. You're walking through the forest and suddenly a sabre tooth tiger (I know, they are extinct, but keep reading) jumps out on the path ahead of you. When this happens, your brain registers a negative emotion – for most of us it's fear. What do you do? You run! Our brains are wired with the 'fight, flight or freeze' response which causes a surge of adrenaline and other stress hormones to pump through your body. This is useful when trying to save your life, but it's doubtful you'll run into a sabre tooth tiger in the world today.

There are however, other stressors that cause your brain to respond to negative emotions in similar ways - shutting off the outside world and limiting the options you see around you.

Some of today's sabre tooth tigers are rush hour traffic, missing a deadline, not exercising after buying that health club membership or having an argument with your spouse. Do events like these pose a real threat to our physical survival? Most likely, not.

Here are two sabre tooth tiger-like examples from my journey. Number one - stressed out about everything you have to get done; finding it hard to actually start anything because you're paralyzed looking at the never ending to-do list. I froze.

Number 2 - feeling bad about not exercising and eating unhealthy foods; all I think about is how little willpower I have, how lazy and fat I've become. I run away from the mirror and the gym and run to the comfort foods on the sofa in my sweat pants.

With each of these examples, my brain closed off to the outside world and focused on the negative emotions of fear, anxiety, and stress — much like it did with the tiger. Negative emotions prevent your brain from seeing the other options and choices that surround you. It's your survival instinct.

Now for the good news…

The benefits of positive emotions don't stop after a few minutes of good feelings. In fact, the biggest benefit that positive emotions provide is an enhanced ability to build skills and develop resources for use later in life. Fredrickson refers to this as the "broaden and build" theory because positive emotions broaden your sense of possibilities and open your mind, which in turn allows you to build new skills and resources that can provide value in other areas of your life.

During my journey, I've learned how to increase positive thinking. Let me share some of the ways to increase you own positive thinking.

Anything that sparks feelings of joy, contentment, and love will work. You probably know what things work well for you. Maybe it's playing the guitar. Maybe it's spending time with a certain person. Maybe it's sitting on your porch in the morning listening to the birds. Here are three ideas for you to consider...

1. Meditation — Recent research by Fredrickson and her colleagues has revealed that people who meditate daily display more positive emotions that those who do not.
Three months after the experiment was over, the people who meditated daily continued to display increased mindfulness, purpose in life, social support, and decreased illness symptoms.

2. Writing — A study, published in the *Journal of Research in Personality*, examined a group of 90 undergraduate students who were split into two groups. The first group wrote about an intensely positive experience each day for three consecutive days. The second group wrote about a control topic.

Three months later, the students who wrote about positive experiences had better mood levels, fewer visits to the health center, and experienced fewer illnesses.

3. Play — Schedule time to play into your life. We schedule meetings, conference calls, weekly events, and other responsibilities into our daily calendars... why not schedule time to play?

Give yourself permission to smile and enjoy the benefits of positive emotion. Schedule time for play and adventure so that you can experience contentment and joy, and explore and build new skills.

Seek joy, play often, and pursue adventure. Your brain will do the rest.

When was the last time you blocked out an hour on your calendar just to explore and experiment?

Take a few minutes right now and write down five things that bring you joy. Come back to your list periodically and add new moments, experiences and joys.

Pretty soon you'll have a nice list to refer back to whenever you need a joy infusion.

4
HOPE

"When the world says, give up.
Hope whispers, try it one more time."

Unknown

I love it when the Olympics are on. We have a front row seat in watching some of the world's greatest athletes compete for a gold medal in their sport. The journey to the Olympics for these athletes are filled with stories of struggle, pain, loss and most importantly hope and the commitment to persevere.

Hope is a vital part of our human existence—the confident belief that there is something more rather than something less, something better instead of something worse, something to live for and invest energy in gives life its necessary depth and meaning and security. **Hope** empowers us to push through incredible obstacles and challenges, to defy the odds and keep going.

Since life, like sport, is messy, full of mistakes and failures, we need hope -- a confidence to carry on. Only those who have hope fight on. Those with little hope fight little. Those with no hope don't fight at all. The Olympic Games offer us a great opportunity to be reminded of some areas that by strengthening in our own lives, can aid us as we pursue our personal and professional goals. Life consistently offers us the opportunity to be successful, however, many times it includes some of the same challenges the Olympians face. It is important for us to persevere through to our goal.

There are eight characteristics that successful athletes stay committed to. Consider including some or all of these focus areas in your lives. The payoff could be as good as or even greater than receiving a gold medal.

• Determination

• Strength

• Hard Work

• Motivation

• Management of Adversity

• Optimistic/Positive Attitude/Hope

• Focus

• Stress Tolerance

Jessie Owens was one of the first African Americans to appear in the Olympics and brought home four gold medals in track and field, against all the odds. When you look at his career, you can see that many of these same focus areas are what enabled him to accomplish greatness.

Jessie Owens said "one chance is all you need." We must consistently position ourselves with all of the preparation and commitment needed to make the most out of a one chance opportunity.

Go out and commit to your goals, your aspirations and go with **Hope!**

5
STRETCH

As the years go by I realize the importance of finding balance, stability and longevity in all aspects of life.

Do I want to be mentally agile and at the top of my game in business, absolutely? Do I want to be as healthy as I possibly can be, yes! Do I want to be fully present in my quiet time and devotion, without a doubt? Do I want to be able to play on the floor and run after grandkids one day, you bet I do! How about YOU?

Recently I was reintroduced to one practice that remains universal to a healthy life and stands the test of time to staying fit physically and mentally for a lifetime – STRETCHING!

There are numerous benefits of stretching. It enhances muscular coordination, Improves posture for better alignment and strengthens muscles. Stretching can lead to a greater sense of well-being, provide relaxation and stress relief and boost mental function. Research also links stretching to WEIGHT LOSS! Stretching also reduces inflammation, Improves performance in physical action, decreases risk of injury, helps joints move through full range of motion and enables muscle to work effectively.

Lydia Di Francesco, a certified Personal Trainer, Nutrition and Wellness Specialist states that even a short amount of time (10-15 minutes) of stretching can calm the mind, provide a mental break, and give your body a chance to recharge.

I realize taking time to stretch our mind, body and spirit may be hard for many of us to do because of today's *busyness*. I reread a post from Rick Warren recently. He spoke about this very thing! He shared his insights by first discussing the book, *Putting the One Minute Manager to Work*, where one of the key concepts is this: Don't Just Do Something—Sit There!

Too often, many of our problems arise from acting before thinking. We confuse activity with productivity. We think, "I'm so busy, I must be accomplishing something!" In reality, we may just be spinning our wheels. Like sitting in a rocking chair, you can expend a lot of energy and create a lot of motion, but you still aren't going anywhere. Progress and productivity always require thought!

Remember, rest and relaxation are important so that the mind and body have time to recuperate. Relaxation that comes through stretching also provides a time for the brain to 'cool down'. Without this time, function and performance decrease and complications arise. Inadequately rested muscles can lead to injury and a tired brain can create stress and confusion. Be sure you are taking enough time to relax and stretch!

6
KINDNESS

Too often we underestimate the power of a touch, a smile, a kind word, a listening ear, an honest compliment, or the smallest act of caring, all of which have the potential to turn a life around

Leo Buscaglia

I received a gift today…a gift of kindness. It wasn't expected or asked for; it wasn't on my wish list or under a tree. It was a kind word, a gentle spirit, a voice sharing her thoughts and validating mine. What an awesome gift.

As I sit to write this afternoon, I keep reflecting on this gift. You've all probably heard about 'random acts of kindness' 'pay it forward' and 'pass it along'. These are just a few of the many discussions around kindness. I wanted to know what else was out there and how kindness impacts our health and overall well-being. Here is what is I found.

David R. Hamilton, Ph.D. shared his work on compassion and kindness in a recent article:

- **Kindness makes us happier** – Elevated levels of endorphins, dopamine creating a "helper's high". A study of more than 3,000 people found that 95% of people feel good when they help someone, 53% of people feel happier and more optimistic, and those feelings last hours or even days for 81% of people.

- **Kindness slows aging** – Kindness/generosity has been linked to release of oxytocin which reduces levels of free radicals and inflammation in the cardiovascular system and thus slows aging at its source. **It's also good for heart!**

- **Kindness makes for better relationships** -We are wired for kindness. Some even say there is such a thing as kindness genes within the human genome. We flourish when we are relational. We are connected through kindness.   Current relationships strengthen and new relationships develop when are kind to one another.

- **Kindness is contagious -** Being kind, inspires others to be kind, creating a ripple effect. My favorite example of this combines my love for coffee and paying it forward. It brings me great joy to get my favorite drink through the drive thru and pay for the next person in line... so many follow suit; that is so cool! I want to challenge you to focus on kindness this month.

Remember, each act of kindness might seem small, but it's actually changing the way we see ourselves, the way we see others, and the way others see us.

How can you make a difference in someone else's life through kindness?

What kind act can you do today for yourself? It's not selfish, it's necessary!

7
STRENGTH

*You gain strength, courage and confidence by every experience in
which you really stop to look fear in the face.*

Eleanor Roosevelt

How many of you love Eleanor Roosevelt? Me too!

What a confident, courageous, and very strong woman she was
and her words still resonate with us today. What does Eleanor have
to do with health and well-being? **STRENGTH!**
Building your strength enhances your health.

We focus on **strength training** with free weights, weight
machines, or resistance bands to help build and maintain muscle
mass and strength. These strong muscles lead to stronger bones. As
one with osteopenia, I know that if I simply add free weights to my
exercising I'd enhance my **health**.

What some may not immediately think about is the power of
strength of character, **strength** in times of adversity and **strength** of
mind on our overall **well-being**.

Dr. Martin Seligman, a leading authority in the field of Positive
Psychology, investigated the relationship between various character
strengths and life satisfaction among 5,299 adults from three Internet
samples using the Values in Action (VIA) Inventory of Strengths.
Consistently and robustly associated with life satisfaction (well-being)
were hope, zest, gratitude, love, and curiosity.

Gallup has been studying human behavior for decades, and all of
its research suggests there is no better place to start than by helping
people become aware of and experience success through more
thoughtful application of their talents and **strengths**.

Eleanor helped so many as First Lady of the United States. She was one of the most outspoken women in the White House. She focused on helping the country's poor, stood against racial discrimination and, during World War II, traveled abroad to visit U.S. troops. After her husband's death, she served at the United Nations, focusing on human rights and women's issues. Even though she faced criticism, adversity and often was disparaged, she was able to face experiences with **strength** and confidence.

What are facing right now that requires your strength? Dig in, find your strength and see what happens.

You can do it!

Do you know your innate strengths (those characteristics that come naturally to you)?

If you're not sure, ask a friend or family member. They can often see in you what you may not see yourself. Learn more about your strengths and cultivate them in different ways each day.

Take a few minutes today and check out VIA Inventory of Strengths. You can take a free survey and find out your top strengths!

8
OVERWHELMED

"Did you hear about the woman found wandering alongside the road? They don't know her name but they know she is a nurse because the back was broken, the ankles were swollen, the nerves were frayed, and the bladder was full"

Unknown

Terrible joke, right? Unfortunately some if it may be true. A recent longitudinal study by Jacobsen and colleagues found that night work and job stress were associated with sleep deficiency, lack of exercise, and increased cardiometabolic risk. Results from another study revealed that hospital-employed bedside nurses have a depression rate of 17% compared to the national rate of 9%. Anecdotally I have heard that fellow nurses often have high blood pressure, muscular/skeletal issues, and unhealthy eating habits. Nurses, the most caring professionals, often fail to care for their own health and wellness.

Many times in my nursing career I have been the poster child for this problem. I'm sure many of you could say the same. As I have matured (another way to say getting old☺) and become more aware of the process of aging I have gained so many insights. Yes, some from the literature but most from my son, Kyle.

A few years back Kyle and I started participating in the Turkey Trot, an annual 5K on Thanksgiving morning. What better way to start the day off before eating 2000+ calories of turkey, dressing, yams, and pies! But seriously, I began to love walking. I then starting running and one Thanksgiving 5K in Charlotte, I actually ran! Now, Kyle ran with me, backwards some of the time to encourage me to keep going, and I did it!

I still continue to get wellness advice from Kyle how to look at food as fuel, how to stretch to reduce injuries, and then there is that ongoing encouragement. I've combined his advice with other expert advice for you.

Listen carefully, we must take care of ourselves. Caring for ourselves will allow us to care for others. I've listed different things I have tried over the years to improve my physical health and overall wellbeing. Choose one, set a goal and start today! You owe it to yourself.

- **Get moving**: Even 5-10 minutes of exercise can boost your energy level.
- **Plan and prepare healthy meals for the week**: Having meals ready and packed saves time and facilitates better choices such as important protein sources coupled with a variety of fruits and vegies.
- **Drink caffeine in moderation**: I'm still working on this one ☹
- **Pause and breathe**: Take a few minutes (2-3 minute break) and practice slow, mindful breathing… breathe in and slowly breathe out a few times. This practice gets oxygen to the brain and allows a moment to refocus, quieten your thoughts and recharge your mind
- **Participate in on-site wellness programs at work**: Some programs offer Tai-Chi and fitness programs, ergonomic training programs, massage, cognitive based therapy, and grief debriefing
- **Practice, practice, practice**: Wellness doesn't happen overnight, but with practice these measures can become habits and habits become a way of life.

Walking remains my favorite exercise. This summer I have renamed it 'hot walking'. It's like hot yoga only its outside, on the walking trail, in 90 to 100 degree weather and 99% humidity! I have added mindful walking to my routine and have pinned this mantra…

"Mind clear, Spirit grateful, Body energized"

What will you choose right now to help clear your mind of all the busyness?

Pick one activity this week to focus on your health; set a goal and start caring for yourself.

Joyful Journey

9
WHAT IF?

*What if…everything you are going through is preparing
you for the next great adventure!*

As I waited for the plane to take me from Orlando and away from
Hurricane Matthew a few months back, I reflected on the past 24-36
hours. Here I was hurrying to get ready for a business trip, catch a
plane, help unpack boxes and begin exhibiting at one of the largest
nursing conference of the year. Only to exhibit for a half day, repack,
get ready to beat a hurricane back to the Carolinas.

Many times in our lives we face obstacles, bumps in the road, or
setbacks that get us off track. And during these times we often begin
to ask ourselves…***What if*…**

"What if I had done this?" or "What if I had listened to so and so?"
or "What if I had left earlier? Or "what if they had canceled the event
sooner?" You get the picture…

All of these *What if* questions started to cloud my thoughts increasing
my doubts and anxiety over the situation. Instead of ruminating on
these questions I deliberately paused, took a deep breath and started
to focus on the bright side.

That is when I noticed the cutest little girl and her mother in the
security line just behind me. The little girl shared a sweet smile and I
smiled back at her and mom. I began a conversation with the mother.
She stated that they were off to Minnesota to spend time with family
while the hurricane came through the east coast. The mother's sweet
child then said, rather proudly, that her Daddy was "staying to help
all the people during the storm". I said, your Daddy must be very

brave. She smiled back at me and shook her head yes. Seeing how brave this little girl and her mom were totally shifted my thinking.

After that brief conversation I began to see this 'setback' as so little in the scheme of things. I shifted to concentrating on the many blessings that were all around me and... *What if?*

I began to savor the time and opportunity:

- To connect with one another and say kind words to other travelers.
- To also see beyond the weather that had us all here together and just smile☺ at those around me
- To engage in conversation and enjoy talking about football while we all waited for a flight (Go DUKE!)...
- To say thanks to all the airport staff who were so hospitable during an otherwise chaotic day for them as well
- To laugh with the ladies who were also traveling back to their homes after the conference was canceled
- To take a selfie on the plane after buckling in to my seat
- To say a prayer for those in the path of Hurricane Matthew

What if ...I had chosen to continue to spiral down with more anxiety and doubt? I would have missed all of those beautiful opportunities.

I'm grateful for a sweet child's smile, her mom and her brave dad who was staying to help all of the people.

Take time today, *right now even*, and notice all of the blessings around you. It can totally shift your mindset☺

10
REFLECTION

Reflection…looking back so that the view looking forward is clearer

Have you taken a moment to reflect on your goals and aspirations? Did you accomplish what you set out to do thus far? What will you focus on during the last six months of the year?

For us to know the answers to these questions, we must pause and reflect. I recently held what I called a midyear retreat to do just that. I left the office, found a quiet place in nature and began reviewing my goals, accomplishments and desired plans for the final months of 2018. I was super excited to see my progress as a nurse entrepreneur and grateful for the opportunities given. I also rediscovered areas that I wanted to pursue and focus on for the rest of the year. This time was necessary for me to know my next moves as a leader.

I recognize that plans don't always follow the projected path. I also understand that when you take time to really look at what you are doing, you can gain clarity and rediscover the purpose of your work.

Bill George, Senior Fellow at Harvard Business School and author of *Discover Your True North* recently discussed contemplative practices that helped him to be a successful leader. Bill noticed that he was chasing everything – 25, 50 objectives all at once. He had no sense of clarity. When he began to pause and meditate, he gained a sense of what was important. He learned to separate the wheat from the chaff and came out of it with the three or four things that he really need to go focus on.

Meditation is but one of several contemplative practices that can enhance your self-awareness.. Others include writing, prayer. talking with someone in great depth or going for a jog to clear your head (save this one for after work). My practice is taking a long walk in nature where I gain clarity and focus.

How do you reflect, rediscover and renew?

Take time daily, weekly, monthly to review your progress? AND celebrate your accomplishments, if only a few moments before moving to the next thing.

When you do…you can celebrate accomplishments, renew goals, and rediscover clarity and purpose!

11
MINDFUL

"The difference between "active" and "busy" is that the former includes reflection
and is directed, whereas the busy life feels out of control and does not seem
purposeful or meaningful."
— Robert J. Wicks

Has this happened to you?

You're washing your hair and you get lost in your thoughts and then you
have to ask yourself…did I use the conditioner already, or not? I can't remember!

Can you relate?

Now some people would say, "Pam, you're getting old; it happens".
While I appreciate the statement, I think it is something else, my
mind is full! Today's world is full of 24/7 information, innovation,
work and other important and not so important stuff.

What have you forgotten recently because your brain was functioning
in 'overwhelm mode'?

When our mind spins without purpose we tend to:

- Let bad things linger and negativity build
- Focus on our mistakes and increase anxiety
- Worry more about how we will get everything done

How does being mindful positively impact our ability to thrive in
today's world? Being mindful is paying attention on purpose in the
present moment with kindness and curiosity. It is being attentive and
aware in the moment. Mindfulness based practices decrease stress,
enhance overall health and increase self-kindness.

The next time you are feeling stressed, overwhelmed or unsure if you conditioned your hair already or not…try this exercise that incorporates several key strategies of mindfulness. Reach for a moment of calm awareness with a mindful **SNACK**.

STOP – *Just stop whatever you're doing.*

NOTICE – *What is happening within and around you?*

ACCEPT – *This is a tricky one. Whatever it is you're struggling with…time, work, skids, sleepiness, frustration…it is what is, accept it for what it is, without judgement*

CURIOUS – *Be curious. Ground yourself with questions about your experience and environment. What am I feeling? What do I need right now?*

KINDNESS – *Respond to yourself and others (mistakes and all) with kindness and observe how that helps things get back on track.*

12
CROSSROADS

There are moments in our lives where we find ourselves at a crossroad, afraid, confused, without a roadmap. The choices we make in those moments define the rest of our days.

I found myself at a crossroad, kicking and screaming, not wanting to let go of anything that I had in my life. I couldn't see that I was overwhelmed, out of time, exhausted, and deeply depressed. I refused to admit that I couldn't do it all. It wasn't until I had to draw a picture of a road that represented my current path and a crossroad where I could follow a new path or stay on the same one.

My therapist then asked me to write on the current path what I was doing every day, how I was feeling each day, when I woke up, how much I slept and what I wasn't doing each day that I really wanted to do. After that exercise, she asked me to focus on the "BOLD reality". She described the BOLD reality as a new path, a new reality for me. I was at a crossroad. It was time for me to make a choice to get my life back.

For a while I just looked at the paper and the empty new path. Did I really have a choice? A choice to slow down and not be afraid of what other people thought. A chance to choose me over everybody else and not feel guilty. What would that look like? Could it be possible?

Little by little the possibilities of my new path began to emerge. I started writing a few ideas on the path – sitting on the front porch of a farm enjoying the sunrise, quiet time with family and friends, more time to walk and enjoy God's gift of nature. As wrote them on the new path I actually began to believe in the possibilities. I drew a sunshine at the beginning of the path, then drew flowers and a few trees along the path. I imagined how I would feel as I walked this new path – relaxed, rested, renewed. I then wrote less time working, less time multitasking and more time single tasking, more time celebrating life, thriving and flourishing each day.

When I finished depicting the BOLD realty on the new path and looked back at the path I was following, I started to cry. I picked up a marker and drew me walking down the old path, tripping, falling and disappearing off the page. Then I picked up another marker and drew myself picking flowers on MY new path. Still crying, but now with joy and not sorrow. I'm moving forward!

A simple activity…profound results!

What does your crossroad look like? Have you looked at the possibilities?

What would you do if you weren't afraid?

13
PURPOSE

Be captivated by purpose.

I woke up one morning with a renewed sense of purpose. I felt light, carefree, unencumbered. This morning I was full of energy and excited about the day's possibilities. Why was this morning different than yesterday or the day before?

I think I know why. Before bed last night I finished a project that had grown so big and unattainable. It wasn't a typical presentation or article about a topic I knew. I had to branch out, expand my knowledge base and create a product from scratch. I didn't feel very confident. I began to doubt my abilities, putting the project off and then the negative self-talk ensued.

"You can't do this; Why did you agree to this? What were you thinking?

Stop! I was not going to go down that road again. For most of my life, I let that little voice in my head tell me I wasn't smart enough, strong enough, and couldn't do it. This negative self-talk kept me from my dreams, my purpose.

I recognized and acknowledged the self-talk, but I also learned to say "not today"!

When you notice feelings and behaviors that haven't served you well in the past, you can stop them in their path. You can face the insecurity and shift your mindset. It takes practice and determination to truly pivot your thinking to a more productive, positive state.

Several skills have helped me move forward and not stumble. First, what triggered the negative self-talk? Second, what thoughts were coming up and why? And third, pause, what response would I choose to make?
I could choose to not listen to that little voice in my head.

I also practice asking myself this question. *What has worked for me in the past to get over a hump and focus on the priority at hand?*

What I found out about myself was I needed to list 3 'must haves' each day. The 'must haves' were my priorities for the day. I was really good at accomplishing tasks on a list. As a matter of fact, I'd do everything on the list and other stuff before tackling the tough stuff. I was an expert procrastinator! By identifying 3 priorities to complete each day, I was able to focus and complete the tough tasks at hand. And guess what, I would feel so accomplished and delighted with myself. Go figure!

The last and most important skill I learned is to follow your purpose, your passion in life.

What inspires you?

What values are important to you and brings meaning to your life?

What is your mission/purpose in life?

Once you establish your purpose/mission in life, you can gauge your actions by saying to yourself (or out loud), am I living my purpose? We each have a purpose in life. This purpose is nurtured by our passions, our values, and our desire to make a difference. Be captivated by your purpose!

14
JOYFUL

In all things, be joyful.

Take delight in your own path, your own journey. Even when you stumble or fall. You can learn so much about yourself with each bend of the road. It won't always be pretty and graceful, but it will definitely make you stronger and more resilient.

With each step gather clarity, strength, and courage. Know that life brings change; be flexible and adapt. Be vulnerable and open to new possibilities.

Make a joyful noise and shout I'm worthy! I'm enough just as I am! Move forward with joyful confidence. The journey for you and me continues!

Consider it all joy.

Joyful Journey

ABOUT THE AUTHOR

Pamela Spivey is an Advanced Practice Registered Nurse and founder of Spivey Consulting, LLC. She shares her 35 years of expertise in nursing and leadership development as a national speaker, author, and certified leadership coach. Pam launched her own business in 2015 to support individual clients and corporate teams through professional coaching, leadership development, and consultative services. Her unique experiences and passion for caring drives her to "help people away from the wall and toward their possibilities".

Pamela resides in North Carolina with her husband and sweet pets, Cinnamon and Katie.

Joyful Journey

56381562R00029

Made in the USA
Columbia, SC
24 April 2019